D0676078

Public Record Office
Pocket Guides to Family History

Getting Started in Family History

Using Birth, Marriage and Death Records

Using Census Returns

Using Wills

Using Army Records

Using Navy Records

GETTING STARTED

in FAMILY HISTORY

PUBLIC RECORD OFFICE

Public Record Office
Richmond
Surrey
TW9 4DU

© Crown Copyright 2000

ISBN 1 873162 87 1

A catalogue card for this book
is available from the British Library

Front cover: ladies skating with 'Lucky Dog',
25 January 1892 (PRO COPY 1/407)

Printed by Cromwell Press Ltd, Trowbridge, Wilts.

CONTENTS

INTRODUCTION	7
STARTING OUT	8
Ask the family	8
Research at home	8
Ten first steps in family history	12
Researching your family name	14
Initial research steps	16
SUMMARY OF RECORDS AVAILABLE	18
Civil registration	18
Parish registers	22
Nonconformist registers	26
– Major collections of nonconformist registers	27
– Detecting nonconformist ancestors	29
Census returns	30
Wills and probate records	34
International Genealogical Index	37
– FamilySearch	38
Family history on the internet	39
Scottish family history	40

Irish family history   42

Welsh family history   46

ORGANISATIONS FOR FAMILY HISTORIANS   47

Public Record Office (PRO), Kew   48

– What to take with you to the PRO   51

Family Records Centre (FRC)   52

Local resources   55

– Local record offices   56

– County and borough library services   57

Family history societies   59

Family History Centres   59

Society of Genealogists (SoG)   60

EMPLOYING SOMEONE ELSE   62

FURTHER READING   63

INTRODUCTION

Genealogy used to be the preserve of the very wealthy, who would trace their noble lines right back to the mythical knights of the dark ages. The ancient Romans even traced their families back to the gods! Now the records and facilities exist for anyone to have a go at tracing their family tree, and nearly everyone who tries will have a measure of success, following their family line back into the 19th century and perhaps earlier.

This Pocket Guide contains everything you need to know to make a start in researching your family history. It suggests where to begin and where to go. It explains the basic skills you will need to acquire in order to search. It describes the range of resources available to help you choose the most suitable for you. It gives you useful information and tips. Researching your family tree is not something to do in a couple of weeks or even a couple of months. It is an absorbing pursuit, which can lead to many years of study if you want to go that far. It is, in fact, one of the fastest growing leisure pursuits in the UK. Who knows, you might find you come from a noble line after all!

STARTING OUT

Ask the family

If you sit down and think about it, you probably know a great deal about your family history already – and this is the first thing to do. It is best to make a written record of everything you know because facts that seem trivial at first might become very important later on. See the check-list of first steps on pp. 12–13.

Research at home

The range of material that you might find at home is extensive. The most obviously valuable records are official documents because they are the most reliable for accuracy:

- Civil registration documents (see p. 18) will give you firm dates of births, marriages and deaths as far back as 1837. They also contain family addresses and an indication of occupation.

- Official army, navy and air force records contain a wealth of reliable information, ranging from dates of birth and addresses to detailed descriptions of personal appearance. There can be few people alive today whose families have not been involved in either the First or Second World War so you are relatively likely to find some sort of military record at home.

- Many people have kept their certificates of qualifications. These will give accurate information about names and ages at the very least.

- Any records you find of membership of a professional body, trade union, etc. can open up a line of research in the records kept by those institutions.

- If your family owned a business you could find interesting records have been kept of it.

- Usually people choose family members as executors for their wills, so you may find records relating to these have been kept. As well as details of the deceased, wills also often include names and addresses of a number of family members because they are most often the beneficiaries and executors.

- More unusual events that you could find documented at home include immigration, criminal and civil litigation, and changes of name by deed poll.

Apart from the reliable facts that can be gleaned from documents there is a lot of information to be deduced from other types of memorabilia. For this you will need to take an analytical approach and also collect clues like a detective. Some of the things you might find are listed below:

- **Photographs**. These can yield more information than you think, even if you don't know the names of the people pictured. For instance, a group of four women

Family photographs can give you valuable clues.
Mr W. Pilkington in mayoral robes, 20 April 1892
(PRO COPY 1/408)

looking alike could be sisters. Can you guess from their clothes when the photograph could have been taken? If you come across the name of one young woman for the right period, you will know to look for her sisters. A man you don't know might be pictured in uniform. Finding this uniform in a reference book will lead you to the correct records to search. Or perhaps you've got a whole series of family photographs that you can't place except that they were all developed in Chelmsford during the 1920s. Then you can check whether a branch of your family moved to Chelmsford.

- **Diaries**. The value of these in family history depends entirely on the character of the people who wrote them and you will have to form a judgement about the reliability of what has been written. Some people keep detailed and meticulous records of the important events in their lives and those of their families. Others neglect their diaries for ages, and then fill them in from memory, which is not always a very accurate way to do it.

- **Bibles**. Many families recorded major events in the front or back of their family Bibles. Remember, though, that accuracy in recording birthdays and ages and consistency in spelling proper names are largely 20th century phenomena.

- **Medals, awards and uniforms**. These all identify a soldier or sailor and can open up a rich avenue of research. You need to record regiment, rank and number if you can find them.

Ten first steps in family history

1. Note all the dates and events you are certain of concerning your immediate family.

2. Start with yourself and your siblings and work back methodically through parents and grandparents as far as you can go.

3. Ask as many people in your family as possible for their recollections and make a separate note of what each person says, so that you can make comparisons.

4. Ask your more knowledgeable or receptive relatives to go over their reminiscences as many times as possible. Nobody ever recalls everything of use in one sitting.

5. Beg and search for as many family records and memorabilia as possible.

6. Have a look in your attic – and ask your elderly relatives if you can look in theirs. People are prone to forget what is stashed in their attics.

7.   Scour the records you find for clues and make a note of any firm information you find together with where you found it.

8.   Show anything you find to your elderly relatives. You may jog a whole stream of fresh memories.

9.   Form a list of questions arising out of your researches so far. This will be the starting point of your research.

10. Don't despair if you can't find out much. The minimum information you need to get started is your own place and date of birth.

Once you have gathered and analysed all the available information at home, you should be able to draw up a list of questions concerning your family's past. It is probably best to choose one line to research at a time, i.e. your mother's or your father's, otherwise your efforts will be spread too thinly and you might quickly get frustrated and give up. Once you have chosen which line to start with it is best to open up your search on a number of fronts. This is partly because you may achieve success more quickly this way and partly because some lines of enquiry take a little time to bear fruit so you need something to do while you're waiting. The table on pp. 16–17 suggests some of the most likely first routes to take.

Researching your family name

It is worth investigating at a fairly early stage what research other people have done into your family name. This might save you a lot of effort if you come across someone who is closely related to you, and at least will put you in touch with experienced researchers and people with similar interests, who may be able to help you out.

ⓘ **Remember**
It is never safe to assume that a family researched by someone else is your family, even if the surname has the same spelling and the family lived in the right area. You must still work back on your own family until you can prove the link.

There are several ways to find people researching the same name:

- **On the internet.** A search on your family name, especially if you associate it with a town or area of the country, will throw up a range of useful information. You can find the e-mail addresses of people researching your surname and the website of the local family history society in the area you are interested in.

- *Register of One Name Studies.* This is a listing of the surnames registered by researchers at the Guild of One Name Studies. It is available through the Society of Genealogists (see p. 61 for address details).

- *British Isles Genealogical Register (BIG-R).* This is a microfiche series produced by the Federation of Family History Societies listing surnames being researched in the UK only.

- *National Genealogical Directory.* This is a listing of research interests by surname published annually by M.J. Burchall.

Initial research steps

What you know	Where to go
Only your own date and place of birth	Look for your birth certificate in the civil registration records. This will give you information about your parents that you can follow up.
	Look for a marriage certificate for your parents in the years preceding your birth.
An approximate date of birth (preferably county of birth too)	Look for a birth certificate.
	Look for other siblings in the preceding and following years.
	Look for the parents' marriage date, often not much more than a year before the birth of the eldest child.
A year of death	Look in the indexes to death certificates. These will tell you either age at death or date of birth so you can then look for birth certificates.

What you know	Where to go
The approximate date of a marriage	Look for a marriage certificate. This gives much useful information about bride and groom, and about their parents if they were witnesses.
County of residence of an ancestor living around 1881	Look in the index to the 1881 census, which lists surnames alphabetically by county. You might easily be able to find your ancestor's census return.
An exact address or the name of a small village where your ancestor lived	These make it easier to find a census return.
An army regiment (and preferably rank and number) and approximate date	Most army records are organised by regiment. Another distinction for all services is the difference between officers and other ranks.

SUMMARY OF
RECORDS AVAILABLE

There are vast resources available for finding out about your family history – enough for a lifetime of searching. One thing they nearly all have in common, though, is that they were not collected with the family historian in mind. The majority of records naming individuals over the centuries have been compiled by institutions connected with government. They were organised according to the purpose for which they were collected rather than to make it easy to find an individual. This can make family history a bit of a detective game. Luckily many indexes have now been compiled (often by volunteers) to help you with your search. This section explains the main types of record and the indexes to them that are available to family historians in the UK and how to make best use of them.

Civil registration

Civil registration is the system still in operation today for recording every birth, marriage and death that occurs in the UK. Civil registration began in 1837 in England and Wales, 1855 in Scotland and 1864 in Ireland. At the beginning there was a certain amount of resistance to the idea of registration and it did not become a legal requirement until 1875, so the comprehensive coverage we take for granted today was only gradually achieved. Nevertheless, with a little persistence, you stand a good chance of finding many of your relatives' registration details from the Victorian period onwards, and these dates and other details of the major events of their lives will form the basic shape of your family tree.

For the purposes of registration, the British Isles were divided into registration districts the same size roughly as a medium sized town. In densely populated cities such as London registration districts were smaller, and in sparsely populated country areas they were larger. The registers were compiled roughly in the order that the events (births, marriages and deaths) occurred, although births and deaths could be registered a few weeks after they took place. Most marriages were registered in church as part of the ceremony.

The actual civil registers are not available to the public for consultation. Searching is done through the indexes to the records, copies of which can be consulted at various locations, as set out on p. 21. There are separate indexes for births, marriages and deaths and they are all arranged by year, with one book for each quarter of the year. In order to make your search you need to know already:

- surname (though the spelling of this might vary)

- approximate date of the event you are looking for

- place where the registration is likely to have occurred

The entries within each quarter are listed alphabetically by surname and then Christian name. Babies unnamed at the time of registration appear at the end of their surname entry in the birth registers. Each entry gives accurate names and dates and indicates in which district the registration took place. In this arrangement people with identical names crop up quite frequently, so it can be difficult to be sure which is the entry you are looking for. The simplest test for this is to check whether the event was registered in the part of the country where your ancestors lived. If it was hundreds of miles away then you are probably (though not definitely) not looking at the entry for your ancestor.

ⓘ **Remember**

If you can't immediately find your ancestor in an index, check the other quarters of the year. There are a number of reasons why registration might have been delayed or maybe the date you have is less accurate than you thought.

Each index entry has a unique reference that indicates exactly where the original registration can be found. Once you are sure that you have found the correct entry in an index you can use this reference to apply for a copy of the original certificate (see address on p. 21). The original certificates contain a wealth of information that is of interest to family historians. They can both confirm facts and open up new lines of enquiry. One of the most important pieces of information you can find is an address for your ancestor's family and this can be used to help you search the census records (see pp. 30–34). You can find out more about civil registration certificates in the Pocket Guide *Using Birth, Marriage and Death Records*.

Microfilm or microfiche copies of the indexes to civil registration certificates are widely available for searching at the resources listed below. More information about these resources is given in later sections of this Pocket Guide.

- Local record offices
- Society of Genealogists
- Office for National Statistics at the Family Records Centre
- National Library of Wales, Aberystwyth
- Family History Centres

With the exact references you can order copies of civil registration certificates for a fee from:

▼ General Register Office
  PO Box 2
  Southport
  Merseyside PR8 2JD
  Telephone: 0151 471 4800
  Internet: http://www.ons.gov.uk/

Parish registers

Before civil registration began in 1837, the best source of official records of births, marriages and deaths is the parish registers, which were compiled by the Church of England. The keeping of these registers was begun in 1538, though very few of the early registers survive. Before 1538 there was no official system for recording people's life events in this way so it becomes much harder to trace them.

Each Church of England parish kept a formal register in which all baptisms, marriages and burials that occurred in the parish community were recorded. Sometimes the three types of events were recorded together in order of occurrence and sometimes they were separated into different parts of the book. Transcriptions, known as the bishops' transcripts, were made for the diocesan records collected at the local cathedral.

An important point to remember about the parish registers is that they were far from comprehensive in recording a local population. There was no reason to record any events that lay outside the business of the church. Therefore births were not recorded, only baptisms, which might have been done long after birth or not at all. Also deaths were not recorded, only burials – though most people had to be buried in church graveyards whether they were Anglicans or not. There were many people who were outside the Anglican religious community for a variety of reasons. Mostly they were people of different faiths including Catholics, Jews and nonconformists. The records about these communities are described below.

Surviving parish registers are scattered throughout the UK, so you need to have a good idea of where your ancestors might have lived before you begin your search. Usually the registers have been deposited in the local record office of the county, town or city where the parish they record was situated. Some registers have remained in the care of the Church of England and can be found in their original parishes or in other church archives. If you live in the area where your ancestors lived then your search will be relatively easy. If you live some distance away, it is best to wait until you have amassed a number of queries to be researched at the same time and to plan a visit carefully in advance. Alternatively you may be able to find a local volunteer who will search the records for you. Volunteers can be contacted through local family history societies or on the internet (see pp. 39–40 and 59). Don't try their patience with very general enquiries, though. Stick to a couple of reasonably precise questions.

ⓘ Remember
If you can't find your ancestor's records in the expected parish, try nearby parishes. Your ancestor might have preferred a neighbouring parish church.

There are two ways to find the original registers you are interested in:

- by consulting *The Phillimore Atlas and Index of Parish Registers*

- by telephoning the likely local record office to check. Local record offices are listed in *Record Repositories in Great Britain*, or if you know the precise area you could find the relevant local record office in the telephone directory.

Alternatively it might be more convenient to search the microfilm versions that have been made of many (but not all) parish registers by the Church of Jesus Christ of Latter-day Saints (LDS). The microfilm copies can be ordered at your local LDS Family History Centre (this is explained on pp. 59–60). The largest collection of copies of parish registers in various forms is held at the Society of Genealogists in London (address on p. 61). Always check that the register you are interested in is available before you plan a visit.

Many indexes to the parish registers have been compiled, and this work still continues. Unless you are sure of your facts, the indexes make the best starting point for searching the parish records. They will give you a precise folio (page) number in the specific parish register where an event was recorded. This can save you months of searching. You can find a list of indexes available in *Marriage, Census and Other Indexes for Family Historians*. The three largest are:

- *International Genealogical Index* (see pp. 37–9)

- *Boyd's Marriage Index*. An alphabetical listing of marriages by surname and Christian name organised by county. The index covers seven million marriages, but is not comprehensive. It is held at the Society of Genealogists, and many local county record offices hold microfilms of those parts that are relevant to the local area.

- *Pallot's Marriage Index*. For marriages that took place in parishes within the City of London, 1780–1837 (and some others as well). For a fee you can request a search from Achievements Ltd, 80 Northgate, Canterbury, Kent CT1 1BA.

ⓘ **Remember**
Always check the information you have found in an index in the parish register itself. It is the only way to be sure that you have found your ancestor.

Finding the correct entry in a parish register can be challenging. Apart from any obvious difficulties of places, dates and names, you will find yourself grappling with such problems as old styles of handwriting, varying levels in the efficiency of record keeping, and abbreviated medieval Latin. There are lots of societies and publications to help you with all this, outlined below (see especially pp. 59–63).

Nonconformist registers

'Nonconformist' is the name given to all those who did not embrace the Anglican faith. If your ancestors were nonconformists they were less likely to have their births, marriages and deaths recorded in the parish registers, though some did as a means of making sure that their children were legitimate. When parish registers were begun in the 16th century, nonconformists had to keep their activities secret because their religious beliefs were persecuted. Gradually religious tolerance grew so that by the late 18th century it was possible for the larger nonconformist groups to organise their own records openly.

There are three minor groups of nonconformists for whom large separate collections of records survive:

- **Catholics.** The Public Record Office (see pp. 48–51) holds seventy-seven Catholic registers; others are listed in the *National Index of Parish Registers* (see vol. III, 1974).

- **Jews.** Jewish communities kept their own meticulous records and shunned every attempt to make them hand these records over to central government. Jews were exempted from Lord Hardwicke's Marriage Act 1753, which refused legal recognition to most other nonconformist marriages. Jewish records have largely remained within the community. Their whereabouts are listed in the *National Index of Parish Registers* (see vol. III, 1974).

- **Quakers.** The Society of Friends or Quakers kept secret and detailed registers from 1613. These were compiled in the Quakers' distinctive style using their own system for dating, which is not easily understood by the uninitiated. They were given up to the Registrar General after civil registration began in 1837 and are now held at the Public Record Office in Kew (see pp. 48–51). Digests (summaries) of the registers can be searched for a fee at the following address:

▶ Friends House Library
  Euston Road
  London NW1 2BJ
  Telephone: 020 7388 1977

Major collections of nonconformist registers

Most nonconformists were adherents of various forms of Protestantism. An ecclesiastical census taken in 1851 suggests that a quarter of the population belonged to nonconformist chapels. Those with surviving registers include: Baptists, Bible Christians, Congregationalists or Independents, Countess of Huntingdon's Connexion, Moravians, Presbyterians, Swedenborgians and Wesleyans and other Methodists. Most of their registers were given up to the Registrar General in the mid-19th century so that they could be used to issue official civil registration certificates. They can now be seen at the Public Record Office and the Family Records Centre. Some nonconformist registers that were never handed over can be found in local record offices and others have remained in the

Quaker marriage certificate, 1713 (PRO RG 6/1277)

congregation. You can check for individual registers in the *National Index of Parish Registers*.

Apart from the records made by individual congregations there were two centralised registries set up by nonconformists:

- **Protestant Dissenters' Registry at Dr Williams's Library.** This was set up in 1742 for congregations of Baptists, Independents and Presbyterians living in the London area, but was eventually used by nonconformists from all over the British Isles.

- **Wesleyan Methodist Metropolitan Registry.** This was set up in 1818 for Wesleyans living throughout the British Isles.

The records of these registries are now held at the Public Record Office and can be searched both at the Kew site and the Family Records Centre (see pp. 48–55).

Detecting nonconformist ancestors

- If there is a nonconformist tradition in your family it is worth trying to trace it back to its origin.

- If you can find no baptism or burial records for your family in the parish registers, they may have been nonconformists.

Census returns

The first census took place in the United Kingdom in 1801 and since then a census has been taken every ten years, except in 1941, because of the Second World War. The early censuses were nothing more than a count of people. The first census to collect personal details was in 1841, and after that a few further changes were made to make sure that the count was comprehensive and that enough detail was recorded.

The census is a survey of people staying in individual households or institutions throughout the UK on a specific night. The head of each household or institution completes a standard form giving information about each person staying there overnight. The specific information collected has gradually been expanded, and includes:

- full name
- age (precise ages were not required until 1851)
- marital status
- relationship to head of household (since 1851)
- sex
- occupation
- place of birth (only whether each person was living in their county of birth in the 1841 census)
- medical disabilities (since 1851)
- whether Welsh or English speaking (in Wales only, since 1851)

In order to encourage people to divulge all this detailed information truthfully, the census records are closed for 100 years, except in a very few cases when there is no other possible way for a next-of-kin to establish a legal entitlement. The 1891 census returns are the latest that can be searched until January 2002.

The information available in the census is invaluable to family historians. A census return gives you a picture of your family on census night. You can find new family members, verify ages and dates and gain an insight into the household and its occupations. You can also make a guess from the information given from one census return to the next what has happened in the intervening years. Be careful not to interpret too much, though. Some facts are not what they seem. For instance, beware of the same name being given to a second child after the first has died.

The census returns are organised according to the original districts in which they were collected. The original returns are too fragile to be thumbed by thousands of searchers so they have been microfilmed. In order to avoid a lengthy search you need first to find the exact reference for the microfilm where your ancestor's return is located. There are four easy routes to getting started on this:

- A name index, if there is one. The 1881 census has a complete name index. The 1851 census is quite well covered, too. Other censuses have some name indexes.

- If you already know the name of a small village where your ancestor lived around the time of one of the censuses you can soon find its reference and look through the returns for the whole village until you find a household with the correct surname. Often you will be able to find the right household.

- You can quickly locate the census return for a precise address within a town.

- If you do not have a precise address but you know the county where your ancestor was likely to be living on the night of the 1881 census you can look for him or her in the name index that has been compiled for this census only. It is arranged alphabetically by county so that even if there are a number of possible returns that could be the one you are looking for you should be able to find the right one reasonably quickly.

The basic rule for searching the census is that the more precisely you can locate where your ancestors were living the quicker you can locate them. Precise addresses can often be found in the family copy of the Bible or on a civil registration certificate. If you do not have a precise address do not despair. You may well still find your ancestor's census return but it will take longer. For more advice and a comprehensive list of finding aids on how to search the census records see the Pocket Guide *Using Census Returns*.

Page: 24

The undermentioned Houses are situate within the Boundaries of the

Civil Parish [or Township] of	Municipal Borough of	Municipal Ward of	Parliamentary Borough of	Town or Village or Hamlet of	Urban Sanitary District of	Rural Sanitary District of	Ecclesiastical District of
Epsom			Epsom		Epsom		

No. of Schedule	ROAD, STREET, &c. and No. or NAME of HOUSE	HOUSES Inhabited (In.) Uninhabited (U.), or Building (B.)	NAME and Surname of each Person	RELATION to Head of Family	CONDITION as to Marriage	AGE last Birthday of — Males / Females	Rank, Profession, or OCCUPATION	WHERE BORN	(1) Deaf-and-Dumb (2) Blind (3) Imbecile or Idiot (4) Lunatic
96	Epsom Green		S. Charles	Head	Mar.	34	Society in House Physician	Chelsea Middlesex	
			Sarah Charles	Wife	do.	28	House Keeper	Somerset Park	
			Eliza Child	Serv.	do.		Servant	Catherine Surrey	
			John Laventon	Serv.	do.	21	Groom	Epsom Surrey	
			Walter Wright			14	Coachman	Brighton Sussex	
97	Station	X	Henry Dyer	Head	Mar.	24	Hawker	Clerce do.	
			Mary A. do.	Wife	do.	26		Winterboard Hants	
			William do.	Bro-Mar	do.	22	Ag. Hawker	do. Surrey Sussex	
98	do.	X	Jenny Porter	Head	Wid.	74		Stopham	
			Elizabeth do.	Serv.	do.	74	Ag. Hawker	Sutton Middlesex	
			Mark do.	Son	Unmar.	7		Epsom Surrey	
						3		Lefthill Middlesex	
98	do.	X	Mary A. do.			1		Camberton Surrey	
			Caroline do.	Head	Mar.	22	W. Hawker	Witterham do.	
			Elizabeth B. do.	Wife	do.	23		Sutherton do.	
98	do.	X	Joseph Piper	Head	Mar.	23	Geo Hawker	Colham do.	
			Louisa do.	Wife	do.	11		Farlsen Park	
			Polly do.	Dau.		7		Epsom Surrey	
			James do.	Son		5		Sutton Park	
99	Epsom Street		Matilda Patterson	Head	Wid.	4	Ag. Hawker	Thomas Sutton Surrey	

Total of Houses	1 & 6		Total of Males and Females	12/13			

Note.—Draw the pen through such of the words of the headings as are inappropriate.

1881 census return for Epsom (PRO RG 11/761, f.86ᵛ)

Microfilm copies of the census returns are accessible in a variety of places:

- the Family Records Centre

- local record offices (which frequently hold microfilmed returns for the surrounding area)

- Family History Centres. (The relevant copies must be requested in advance.)

Wills and probate records

A will, despite its legalistic formulation, can give you a real insight into your ancestor's personality and some firm facts too. Wills dating back as far as 12 January 1858 (when a single independent Court of Probate was set up) can usually be easily found. Wills proved before 1858 were dealt with in local courts and are generally more difficult to find. You can find out more in the Pocket Guide *Using Wills*.

There are two separate types of records that are preserved concerning wills and probate. The first concern the will itself and the second concern grants of administration that are made when there is no will or when the executor named in a will is unable to carry out the appointed task. Copies of both original wills and administrations proved after 1858 can be read at the Probate Searchroom (address on p. 36).

In order to locate the exact reference for the documents, you need first to locate them in the indexes to the records. The indexes in themselves give more information than a death certificate about the testator and his family, especially the indexes covering the period 1858–92. There are separate indexes for wills and administrations up to 1870, but from 1871 onwards the two types of records are indexed together.

ⓘ Remember

It can be easier to find your ancestor in the wills index than it is in the civil registration index of deaths.

The original indexes, after 1858, can be searched at the Probate Searchroom. Microfiche copies of them are available at:

- the Public Record Office, Kew
- the Family Records Centre

- the Society of Genealogists

- some District Probate Registries, though most have handed their historical records over to local record offices

- some reference libraries

When you look in the indexes, if you are sure you have found the correct reference for your ancestor's will, there is no need to travel to London to read it. A copy can ordered by post from the Court Service, York Probate Sub-registry, Duncombe Place, York YO1 2EA.

▼ Probate Searchroom
Principal Registry of the Family Division
First Avenue House
42–9 High Holborn
London WC1V 6NP
Telephone: 020 7936 7000

Opening times (closed on bank holidays)

Monday to Friday   10 a.m. to 4.30 p.m

No appointment is necessary, but a charge is made for each will ordered.

The latest time for ordering a will to be read the same day is 3.00 p.m.

International Genealogical Index

The *International Genealogical Index* (*IGI*) is a microfiche index arranged by county of millions of names gathered from records all over the world. It is compiled by the Church of Jesus Christ of Latter-day Saints and updated regularly as more records are added to the database. The greatest part of the information for the index comes from parish registers of baptisms, marriages and deaths, though other records, such as nonconformist registers, have been included too.

The *IGI* is a good starting point if you are searching for an ancestor before civil registration began in 1837, though its coverage extends from the time of the first parish registers in 1538 right up to the mid-1880s. It is useful because:

- it contains names from both nonconformist and parish registers

- you can use it to find people who moved around from parish to parish

Once you have found a relevant entry in the *IGI* it is best to check it in the original register if you can. The original register is likely to contain more detailed information than appears in the *IGI* too.

It has been supplemented recently by the *British Isles Vital Records Index*, on CD-ROM, which can be seen at the Family Records Centre and other places.

> ### ⓘ Remember
> The *IGI* is not comprehensive – not all parish registers are covered at all and some are only partially covered. You can check this to some extent in the separate microfiche listing called *Parish and Vital Records Listings*.

FamilySearch

This is a version of the *IGI* on CD-ROM that also includes data collected by members of the LDS Church. You can use this CD-ROM to find all instances of a specific name in a specific period and it may turn up an ancestor where you would never have expected to find one. Type in everything you know and see what comes up – but remember that there are gaps in coverage. Also you need to be aware of the different possible spellings of surnames, especially as the arrangement of the names is phonetic.

Access to the *IGI* and possibly to *FamilySearch* is available at:

- Family History Centres

- the Family Records Centre

- the PRO at Kew

- the Guildhall Library, Aldermanbury, London EC2P 2EJ; telephone: 020 7332 1862/3

- the Society of Genealogists

- local record offices and libraries, which often hold those parts of the *IGI* that cover the surrounding counties

- on the internet

Family history on the internet

The internet is useful to family historians as a reference tool and as a way to contact other people who share your interests. The large organisations, such as the PRO and the Church of Jesus Christ of Latter-day Saints, have websites that are expanding daily. You can find much information and advice on these sites, and their greatest use is to provide up-to-date information about the scope of their collections and how to access them. You can do some limited searching of the records collections of the LDS Church, but be aware that most of the references that turn up are to American families.

The internet is a good way to make contact with smaller organisations and individuals too. If you type in the name of the county where your ancestors lived then you should be able to find information about the local family history society and a great deal of information about the local area. If you type in your family name you can find the e-mail addresses of others who are interested in researching it. You might find a relative or at least make a friend.

Public Record Office
http://www.pro.gov.uk/

Office for National Statistics
(General Register Office of England and Wales)
http://www.ons.gov.uk/

General Register Office for Scotland
http://www.open.gov.uk/gros/groshome.htm

FamilySearch
http://www.familysearch.org/

Society of Genealogists
http://www.sog.org/

Familia – a reference site for what family history
resources exist in county and borough libraries
http://earl.org.uk/familia/

GENUKI – a reference site for family history in the UK
http://genuki.org.uk/

Scottish family history

The main resource for researching Scottish family history is in Edinburgh at the General Register Office for Scotland (although this resource can be reached via the

Scottish Link at the Family Records Centre in London – see p. 55. The records held in Edinburgh relating to births, marriages and deaths include:

- births, marriages and deaths in Scotland since 1855

- legal adoptions since 1930

- divorces since 1984

- parish registers 1553–1854

- censuses (1881 and 1891)

▼ General Register Office for Scotland
New Register House
3 West Register Street
Edinburgh EH1 3YT
General telephone: 0131 334 0380
Search room telephone: 0131 314 4450
Fax: 0131 314 4400
Internet: http://www.open.gov.uk/gros/groshome.htm

Search room opening times

Monday to Friday   9.00 a.m. to 4.30 p.m.

The cost of a full day of searching is £17. From 1.00 p.m. a charge of £10 is made for any remaining seats. If you are travelling some distance to come and search it is advisable to book your place, but otherwise booking is not essential since a third of the seats cannot be reserved in advance.

Irish family history

In 1922 there was a massive fire at the Irish Public Record Office, which destroyed many of the records that family historians need to search. This makes it very difficult to trace Irish families. The scale of the destruction included:

- half of all surviving Anglican Irish parish registers

- nearly all probate records (though the Society of Genealogists holds a collection of abstracts of Irish wills 1569–1909)

- most census returns

Those records that do survive are split between archives in Northern Ireland and the Republic of Ireland. You can see the location of the major collections of records in the table on pp. 44–5.

The best starting point for researching your Irish ancestors is to contact the

▼ Irish Genealogical Research Society
   82 Eaton Square
   London SW1W 9AJ

who may be able to help. It is also worth checking the *IGI*, which contains information from those few parish registers that remain.

▸ General Register Office of Ireland
  Joyce House
  8–11 Lombard Street
  Dublin 2
  Ireland
  Telephone: 003531 6711863

▸ General Register Office (Northern Ireland)
  Oxford House
  Chichester Street
  Belfast BT1 4HL
  Telephone: 028 9025 2000
  Internet: http://www.nisra.gov.uk/gro/

▸ National Archives of Ireland
  Bishop Street
  Dublin 8
  Ireland
  Telephone: 003531 4072300
  Internet: http://www.nationalarchives.ie/

▸ Public Record Office of Northern Ireland
  66 Balmoral Avenue
  Belfast BT9 6NY
  Telephone: 028 9025 5905
  Internet: http://proni.nics.gov.uk/

Record type	Location (Eire)	Location (Northern Ireland)
Births, marriages and deaths for the whole of Ireland 1864–1921 and for Eire since 1864	General Register Office of Ireland	General Register Office of Ireland
Births, marriages and deaths in Northern Ireland since 1 January 1922		General Register Office of Northern Ireland
Non-roman Catholic marriages since 1845	General Register Office of Ireland	General Register Office of Ireland
Census returns 1821–1911	National Archives (Dublin)	National Archives (Dublin)

Record type	Location (Eire)	Location (Northern Ireland)
Census returns 1926 (Eire only)	National Archives (Dublin)	
Applications for old age pensions 1908–22	National Archives (Dublin)	Public Record Office of Northern Ireland
Calendars of all wills proved and administrations granted since 1858	National Archives (Dublin)	Public Record Office of Northern Ireland

Welsh family history

A unique feature of Welsh family history is that there was no convention of having a fixed surname until comparatively recently (17th to 18th centuries) and even then there was little variety in the range of surnames taken. This gives researchers of Welsh family history their own particular problems and means that they need to study Welsh naming traditions.

Apart from this problem there is little practical difference between searching for Welsh ancestors and searching for English ancestors since the records are derived from the same system. A useful resource for those researching Welsh family history is the National Library of Wales. This library holds a large collection of records and finding aids, some of which are general and some specifically relevant to Wales including:

- indexes to the civil registers 1837–1983

- census returns for Wales 1841–91

- *IGI*

- Welsh parish registers

- Welsh diocesan records

- Welsh nonconformist records

- wills and administrations from local Welsh courts

▼ The National Library of Wales
 Aberystwyth
 Ceredigion SY23 3BU
 Telephone: 01970 632800
 Fax: 01970 632883
 Internet: http://www.llgc.org.uk/

Opening times (closed Sundays, Bank Holidays and first full week in October)

Monday	9.30 a.m. to 6 p.m.
Tuesday	9.30 a.m. to 6 p.m.
Wednesday	9.30 a.m. to 6 p.m.
Thursday	9.30 a.m. to 6 p.m.
Friday	9.30 a.m. to 6 p.m.
Saturday	9.30 a.m. to 5 p.m.

ORGANISATIONS FOR FAMILY HISTORIANS

As you can see from the above, there are many ways to go about searching for your family history. In the early stages your choice will depend partly on where you live, partly on how much time you can spare and partly on the type of information you have already gathered. This section lists the organisations mentioned in the text and gives basic information about them and the records they hold.

Public Record Office (PRO), Kew

The Public Record Office is the national repository (store-house) for government records in the UK. Its main site at Kew holds the surviving records of government back to the Domesday Book (1086) and beyond. The largest proportion of the records are English and Welsh. Scotland and Northern Ireland have their own record offices but the PRO does hold some Scottish and Irish records too. There are also records relating to the British Empire.

The PRO has a vast wealth of records available for research. The records already occupy more than 170 km of shelving and are increasing every day. Of course many types of record are not of special interest to family historians. The previous sections of this book have mentioned many that are. In addition it is worth mentioning that the PRO Kew site is usually the best place to go if you wish to search for an ancestor in the armed forces. You can find out more about the full range of relevant records accessible at Kew in A. Bevan, *Tracing Your Ancestors in the Public Record Office*.

There is also an extensive library at Kew, with a unique collection of books and periodicals on family history as well as other aspects of history. One of the most important collections is of the publications of local records societies.

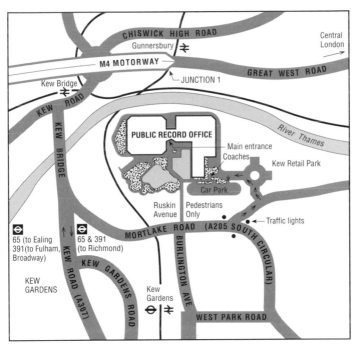

How to find the Public Record Office, Kew

▼ Public Record Office
Kew
Richmond
Surrey TW9 4DU
General telephone: 020 8876 3444
Telephone number for enquiries: 020 8392 5200
Telephone number for advance ordering of documents
(with exact references only): 020 8392 5260
Internet: http://www.pro.gov.uk/

Opening times (closed Sundays and Bank Holidays)

Monday	9.00 a.m. to 5 p.m.
Tuesday	10 a.m. to 7 p.m.
Wednesday	9.00 a.m. to 5 p.m.
Thursday	9.00 a.m. to 7 p.m.
Friday	9.00 a.m. to 5 p.m.
Saturday	9.30 a.m. to 5 p.m.

No appointment is needed to visit the PRO in Kew, but you will need a reader's ticket to gain access to the research areas. To obtain a ticket you need to take with you a full UK driving licence or a UK banker's card or a passport if you are a British citizen, and your passport or national identity card if you are not a British citizen. Note that the last time for ordering documents is 4 p.m. on Mondays, Wednesdays and Fridays; 4.30 p.m. on Tuesdays and Thursdays, and 2.30 p.m. on Saturdays.

What to take with you to the PRO

- £1 coin (refundable) to leave any extra baggage in a locker

- money or a credit card if you are intending to buy copies of any records

- pencil (ink and rubbers are not allowed at Kew in case they damage original records, but they are allowed at the FRC)

- paper to record what you find (notebooks are allowed at both the FRC and Kew, but at Kew no more than 6 loose sheets are permitted)

- a record of any research you have done so far to make sure you don't go through anything twice unnecessarily

- a laptop computer if you wish.

Family Records Centre (FRC)

The Family Records Centre is a service for family historians set up in 1997 by the Office for National Statistics (ONS) and the Public Record Office. It gathers together a range of resources and research facilities specifically designed with family historians in mind. The holdings of the ONS at the FRC include:

- births, marriages and deaths in England and Wales since 1 July 1837

- legal adoptions in England and Wales since 1927

- births, marriages and deaths of some British citizens abroad since the late 18th century, including deaths in the two World Wars

- births and deaths at sea July 1837–1965

- regimental records 1761–1924, army chaplains' returns, and armed service registers of births, marriages and deaths 1796–1965

- civil aviation births and deaths 1947–65

- registers of Ionian Islands births, marriages and deaths 1818–64

On the first floor of the FRC the holdings of the PRO include microfilm of:

- census returns 1841–1891

- death duty registers 1796–1858, indexes 1796–1858

- wills and administrations of the Prerogative Court of Canterbury, 1383–1858

- many nonconformist registers 1567–1837

- miscellaneous foreign returns of births, deaths and marriages 1627–1960

▼ Family Records Centre
1 Myddelton Street
London EC1R 1UW
General telephone: 020 8392 5300
Telephone for birth, marriage and death certificates:
0151 471 4800
Fax: 020 8392 5307
Internet: http://www.pro.gov.uk/
ONS website: http://www.ons.gov.uk/

Opening times (closed Sundays and Bank Holidays)

Monday	9 a.m. to 5 p.m.
Tuesday	10 a.m. to 7 p.m.
Wednesday	9 a.m. to 5 p.m.
Thursday	9 a.m. to 7 p.m.
Friday	9 a.m. to 5 p.m.
Saturday	9.30 a.m. to 5 p.m.

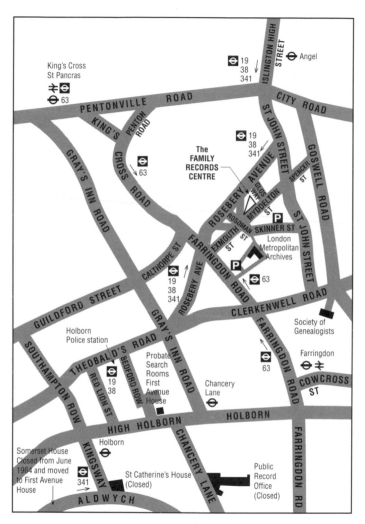

How to find the Family Records Centre

You can visit the FRC in person without an appointment at the opening times shown in the table. When you have found a reference for a civil registration certificate you can order a copy directly at the FRC using forms available at the information desk. Copies are available for collection after four working days or can be sent to you by post. If you are unable to visit the FRC yourself you can order certificates by post, fax, telephone or using the internet. You can also make copies of any census returns and most wills that you find during the course of your researches.

A Scottish Link is also available at the FRC. Here you can book a computer for up to two hours at a time to search online the main genealogical sources (outlined under Scottish family history on pp. 40–41) for Scottish ancestors and order copies of birth, marriage and death certificates. A fee is charged to use this online service and it is advisable to book time in advance. Telephone 020 7533 6438 to make a booking.

Local resources

If you are lucky enough to live in the area where your ancestors lived before you there is a great deal of research that you can do locally either before or at the same time as you launch on the central government records.

Local record offices

Every county in the UK has a local record office that you can find in the telephone directory, and many local record offices are linked to the local central library. A full list of local record offices can be found in *Record Repositories in Great Britain.*

Local record offices hold many types of record that are inaccessible elsewhere including:

- original parish registers for the local area

- wills proved in the local church courts before 1858

- other local court records

- a range of other possible parish records, mostly to do with the relief of the poor

- local government records including property and taxation records and electoral registers

- local business records

- local school records and sometimes records of apprentices

- local maps and directories, which can be indispensable when you are looking for an exact address

- local newspapers, which might include your ancestor in an exciting story or more likely in the births, marriages and deaths announcements or the regimental information published in newspapers during the First and Second World Wars

- unpublished indexes and finding aids that have been compiled locally

Copies of the national records, such as census returns, that apply to the local area have also often been purchased where available so it is quite possible to trace many families back for centuries in local record offices, so long as they remained within the locality.

Before you visit a local record office it is wise to contact it first to find out when it is open and whether it is likely to contain the information you are looking for. If you cannot make a visit yourself it is possible to write asking a specific question, but don't ask for too much help because the staff do not have a remit for extensive searching on your behalf. If you have a number of questions it is advisable to contact a volunteer or paid searcher. You can do this through the local family history society or via the internet.

County and borough library services

Many library services now offer two things which will be of great value to you: access to the internet, and their own collections of material for family and local history. You may not find these at a branch library, but you should at the central library.

Access to the internet will bring many sources for family history much closer to hand. Some internet addresses have been given in this Pocket Guide – there are *very* many more websites on family history.

To find out what sources are available near you, you need to access a service on the internet called *Familia* (http://www.earl.org.uk/familia/). This is a directory of family history resources held in public libraries in the UK and Ireland. Each library has provided information on whether they hold any of the following:

- Registrar General's indexes to births, marriages and deaths from 1837 (England and Wales) or from 1855 (Scotland)

- parish registers, 16th to 20th centuries

- *International Genealogical Index*

- census returns 1841–1891

- directories 18th to 20th centuries

- electoral registers and poll books 18th to 20th centuries

- unpublished indexes

- newspapers

- periodicals

- photographs

Family history societies

Joining a local family history society can help you directly in tracing your family history as well as being fun. You could join the society that is local to where you live or the one that covers the area where your family lived – or both!

Family history societies give you access to the experience of others and the opportunity to attend meetings and learn new skills. You can also advertise your interests in their journals. Much of the important indexing work that makes records accessible to the general public is done voluntarily by members of family history societies, and the finding aids that they produce are often deposited in the relevant local record offices.

Many family history societies have their own websites on the internet or you can find out more by contacting:

▼ The Federation of Family History Societies
  Benson Room
  Birmingham and Midland Institute
  Margaret Street
  Birmingham B3 3BS

Family History Centres

The Church of Jesus Christ of Latter-day Saints (Mormons) has set up a number of Family History Centres throughout the UK linked to a central genealogical library located in Salt Lake City, Utah in the United States of America. Each Family History Centre has a copy of the *IGI* and *FamilySearch* (described in separate sections on pp. 37–9 above) and copies of the 1881 census index. You can also gain access there to millions of records compiled by members of the Church. In addition you can request for a fee a huge range of microfilm and microfiche copies of genealogical records which are held in the library in Salt Lake City.

If you live near a Family History Centre, you can save yourself a great deal of travel by doing your research there. You do not have to be a member of the Church. For more information write to:

▶ The Genealogical Society of Utah
   British Isles Family History Service Centre
   185 Penns Lane
   Sutton Coldfield
   West Midlands B76 8JU

Society of Genealogists (SoG)

If family history is set to become an important hobby for you then you will find it worthwhile to join the Society of Genealogists. This society runs courses in genealogy for beginners and publishes a quarterly magazine and a wide range of books on family history.

The library at the Society of Genealogists contains a large collection of records and finding aids, some of which are unique. The library covers Scottish and Northern Irish records as well as English and Welsh and has much on local history as well as genealogy. It has the largest collection of copies of parish registers in the UK and also has an extensive collection of family histories and one-name studies. Through the Society of Genealogists you can contact the Guild of One Name Studies, which publishes annually a list of names being studied.

You do not have to be a member of the Society of Genealogists to use its library, although you do have to pay a fee. You can visit it without an appointment. It is conveniently located for you to combine a trip there with a trip to the FRC.

▼ Society of Genealogists
   14 Charterhouse Buildings
   Goswell Road
   London EC1M 7BA
   Telephone: 020 7251 8799
   Internet: http://www.sog.org.uk/
   Opening times (closed Sundays and Mondays)

Tuesday	10 a.m. to 6 p.m.
Wednesday	10 a.m. to 8 p.m.
Thursday	10 a.m. to 8 p.m.
Friday	10 a.m. to 6 p.m.
Saturday	10 a.m. to 6 p.m.

EMPLOYING SOMEONE ELSE

It isn't always convenient or cost effective to do all the research yourself. Some record offices provide a research service, and will do work for you for a fee. The Public Record Office and the Family Records Centre cannot do research for people, and expect you to come yourself or ask someone to come for you.

Many independent researchers exist who will search records and provide copies for a fee. To be sure of high standards choose a paid researcher from the *List of members* of the Association of Genealogists and Record Agents. The list is available from the Society of Genealogists, who also give good advice on what to expect (address on p. 61). A list of independent researchers is also available on the PRO website, or by phone.

FURTHER READING

D. Begley, ed. *Irish Genealogy: A Record Finder* (Dublin, 1982)

A. Bevan, *Tracing Your Ancestors in the Public Record Office* 5th ed. (PRO, 1999)

J. Cox and S. Colwell, *Never Been Here Before? A Genealogists' Guide to the Family Records Centre* (PRO, 1998)

J. Gibson and E. Hampson, *Marriage, Census and Other Indexes for Family Historians* 6th ed. (FFHS, 1996)

C.R. Humphery-Smith, *The Phillimore Atlas and Index of Parish Registers* 2nd ed. (Chichester, 1995)

National Index of Parish Registers (Society of Genealogists from 1968 to present)

Record Repositories in Great Britain 11th ed. (PRO/ Royal Commission on Historical Manuscripts, 1999)

J. Rowland and S. Rowlands, *The Surnames of Wales* (FFHS, 1996)

D.J. Steel and E. R. Samuel, *Sources for Roman Catholic and Jewish Genealogy and Family History* (National Index of Parish Registers, vol. III, 1974)